Bob McCluskey

Smooth Rhymes from a Wrinkled Mind

Word Alive Press
131 Cordite Road, Winnipeg, MB R3W 1S1
www.wordalivepress.ca

Cataloguing in Publication may be obtained through Library and Archives Canada

Dedication

I am delighted to dedicate this book of humorous and sometimes irreverent poetry to my family, to Agnes Mary's family, and to all of my friends who have tickled my funny bone over the years. May all of their lives continue to be lived with humor and unyielding commitment to the source I believe, of our humor and indeed, of all our blessings, our Lord Jesus Christ.

Antiderivative

October 20, 2012

Over all of the years
With the smiles and the tears
I have memories
I'd like to relive
I just figured a way
I can do it today
With an antiderivative

I'll start with October
The month that I'm in
Just reverse the disorder
And slowly begin
To walk slightly backward
Through year after year
Forgetting the year that I'm in

I know some new calendars
I'll have to buy
That will not be easy
I'll just have to try But as I go back
Old friends come into view
C'mon, say hello
I just bumped into you

But I'd better be careful
The song that I croon
If I go back too far
I'll reenter the womb
And that won't be funny
I'll just disappear
And won't even remember
That God placed me here

Affairs of State

October, 2009

We live in times so far advanced,
electronically intimidate, world information inundate,
this century communicate to the least of we the
people so entranced,
details of affairs of state intended for the eyes and ears
of Pharaohs, kings, prime ministers in former years,
but not of late.

Our kings seem somehow now unfit.
These possessors of the wherewithal to lead us by this
knowledge,
on their backsides loll, in other words, just sit.

Whereas we proletariat,
who weightily discuss the pros and cons of this and
that,
self-righteously engaging all, engaging us, round water
cooler vat.

This plethora of information saturates our
overburdened brain.
To weigh us down, we who should lead, to be
responsible you know, to settle world affairs in
perpetuity, however vain.

We fathers and grandfathers, octogenarian wise,
pontificate with greatest depth of gravity,
as from computer and TV, surmise,
the consequences of increased depravity.

We are responsible, to large decisions make.
Like repairing the economy, or starting a war, or
holding elections now.
Small decisions to our wives we delegate,
it's only fair they do their share, somehow.

Like sell the house or not, or trade the car, or food or
dress,
or doctors, dentists, school and such, social finesse.
Relieving us to greater things attend, resolve we must
our country's woes, as home we wend, i.e. financial
trust,
our nations spending altogether much too much.

But now I'm home, at last arriving ere I starve.
whatever will we have to eat, why lovely prime rib
roast, a treat,
thank you, my dear, I'll carve.

Aging Time

August 18, 2012

Fresh revelation aging brings
of all that passed before in life.
Values change with rearrange
of time's demands, of little things.
Somehow unimportant now.
Somehow.

Ones mind that once was taken up
with life's demands in symphony.
Too much to do, too little time,
with never quite enough supply,
to meet the needs imposed on me,
always racing to catch up, to wonder why,
as time flew by.

No race to run, no clock to beat,
responsibility is gone.
It used to be, they'd look to me
to wrap each problem up complete.
I'd solve them all with great aplomb
while madly running off my feet.
That day is gone.

For that is all behind us now,
our race is run, our die is cast.
We stop to smell the roses now,
or contemplate the couch at last.
While others race to beat the clock,
our hand's no longer on the plough
seems strange, somehow.

Agnes Mary Martin's Eighty-Fifth Birthday

January 16, 2010

I called on Agnes Mary Martin
on her special day,
to see if Agnes Mary Martin
could come out to play.

Agnes Mary Martin said
it's probably all right,
her family said, but only if
she's home while it's still light.

That's okay by me, I said,
'cause where we're gonna be,
we'll need daylight and sunshine
all the butterflies to see.

We'll both be skipping gaily
through the meadow fields and then,
we'll tip-toe through the sunbeams
in a flowered cathedral glen.

We'll picnic with the honeybees
in nature's lovely bowers,

and gladly share with honey bear,
sweet nectar from God's flowers.

When Big Ben strikes the hour, then
we'll know it's time to flee,
I'll set the pace as home we race,
and have her back by three.

Angelina Ant

November 29, 2012

If e'er you've read my second book,
A reference there you'd see,
To Charles the ant, now not extant,
He lived in rhyme, but now he can't,
Lost now to history.

My name is Angelina Ant,
Sweet Charlie Ant and me,
Were lovers once upon a time,
I was his and he was mine,
In silly poetry.

I had the slimmest waist in town
And largest derriere.
So large it's always falling down,
In Antville 'twas of great renown,
None other could compare.

But then one day my tiny waist
Abruptly broke in two.
To walk about would be bad taste,
my derriere had gone to waste,
I hide now, wouldn't you?

For now I'm only half an ant
I've nothing on behind
Wish Charles were here, I know he can't
He'd love me, though recalcitrant
And wouldn't ever mind

Though I'm not the ant I used to be
Half an ant is better than none
What's left is only the half that eats
But Charles I know would buy me treats
Even though I'm half undone
I miss you, Charlie!

Aphorisms

January 25, 2010

I know that love's the answer,
it's the question puzzles me,
comedy or humor's just
a funny way to serious be.

A conscience clear, remember dear,
reflects a memory short,
if the habit make, to truth relate,
your memory can abort.

Don't bury your talents,
for use they were made,
of what use is a sundial
if left in the shade.

Remember it's God
brings the healings we see,
but the physician's submission
will garner the fee.

A new baby's God's opinion,
the world should ever be,
as she ages though,
her beauty will steal inward,
by degree.

Modern man they say,
is the missing link,
between apes
and human beings, I think.

If in magic you've purposed
to never believe,
then who pops up the
next Kleenex
to put in your sleeve.

Don't ever go faster
than the speed of light,
else your hat will blow off
as you speed through the night.

A man wrapped up in himself
small package will make,
dare you open that package,
might be a mistake.

Lots of money is better
than poverty, I know,
but only for
financial reasons though.

A diplomat might remember
a woman's birth date,

but to reveal her age,
he'll not publicly state.

Anyone to a psychiatrist,
thinks he must go,
Should have his head examined,
don't you know.

My truth's more important
than anything,
So the facts that confuse me,
please don't bring.

In the very same language,
everyone smiles,
So a humorous outlook
will carry you miles.

And the only living
creature, to blush, ever can,
is the only creature who
should, namely, man.

An eye for an eye,
man responding in kind,
does that mean the whole
world has to end up blind.

All this humor I'd sooner
create on my own, but I just do the
rhyming, please let it be known.

Attentive Angels

October 6, 2011

There are angels they say,
watching every day,
who are instant, in season and out.
in a moment may fly,
much too quick for the eye,
to save ere we even shout.

Now I know this is true,
and perhaps also, you
are aware of examples from life.
When she tripped as she entered,
pitched forward off centered,
an angel uprighted my wife.

But the thought that occurred,
when this story I heard,
they must pay undivided attention.
Watching with a keen eye,
seem to not even try,
with their non-accidental prevention.

When I'm ever alone,
must admit I am prone,
to relieving rude physical angst.
When I get that old itch,

that subliminal glitch,
I don't want angels watching, no thanks.

They must really amaze,
when our antics they gaze,
I am very embarrassed to think.
I was stripped to the buff,
and if that ain't enough,
I was washing my feet in the sink.

So the end of this tale,
modesty must prevail,
henceforth use impeccable habit.
When in shower I grope,
end up dropping the soap,
I will never bend over to grab it.

Bold Knight's Defeat

August, 2009

Bold knight valiant takes the field seeks victory this
day.
Worthy foe will force to yield, intimidate with lance
he'll wield to enter into fray.

Our knight, prancing, snorting, as
the enemy engage.
Strike fear with deadly lance he's sporting,
round his foe with pride cavorting,
sweet victory presage.

Alas, knight's worthy foe unhorse
to lie with no defence.
At disadvantage now, of course,
to fear defeat, or something worse,
knight's sport will now commence.

Leaning over victim, proudly lance reveal
to now engage.
This worthy foe is soon to feel
the entrance of knights' lance of steel
at center stage.

As knight indulged another glance,
his foe sensed victory.

In that moment took a chance,
both hands surround knight's threatening lance,
held on with a look of glee.

They struggled for a while this way,
foe strong with victory stroke.
First one, then other one held sway,
but bold knight lost, to his dismay,
exhausted fell...lance broke.

Foe delighted, ran away
to music room nearby.
Sweet melody on organ play,
inspired by the noisome fray,
recovered with a sigh.

Careless Youth

May 1, 2011

Ah! Careless youth unknowing
Gaily going through each day
Extravagantly lavishing
Times currency away
The time they own
Is all their own
To squander as they will
Or so they say
Whilst every day
That day is gone until
The bag of golden days
That was allotted
Dwindles down
Days into months
Months into years
Till one day with a frown
The lovely loose and limber
Joints and tendons
Now are sore
Those careless exercisings
Aren't working anymore
So who am I
I hear you cry
What gives me the right
To chasten you

I have the right
Because it's true
Each day I'm blue
And hurting every night.

Chance Meeting

February 15, 2011

How come when we meet, we say "How ya doin"
when really, we couldn't care less.
Oh, I guess we do care, but that's not what we mean,
we just mean "hello," when acquaintance is seen,
it's a lifetime of habit, I guess.

Now, that friend that we meet thinks we mean what
we say,
that our interest elicits reply.
He then casts about in his mind to give out,
all his physical problems plus others no doubt,
while we're wiping a tear from our eye.

Then at last when we part with an impatient start,
we exhale a great sigh of relief.
Nothing personal mind, it's just that we find,
we feel bored to tears, but we want to be kind,
so much better when meetings are brief.

And not only that, in the midst of our chat,
I too had a great deal to say.
My problems are many and major, you know,
it would have been great to have told him so.
I was speechless as he walked away.

When I think of it now, he seemed burdened
somehow,
I guess it was all for the best.
He just needed somebody to listen, to hear,
it was good that we met, I could lend him my ear,
as he got it all off of his chest.

Chronological Angst

June 16, 2011

How carelessly youth, when they get out of bed,
arrange their coiffeur with a shake of the head.
How flawless and faultless their visage display,
as they play every night, work or school every day.

Quite well seasoned, well reasoned, arrive middle age,
while sporting, contorting, with workouts engage.
There is naught to portend life's oncoming decline,
as they're prancing, romancing while dancing the line.

Then one quick turnaround, to their utter dismay,
they've arrived at the age of organic decay.
Now a salve is for this and a pill is for that,
everyone is too heavy, a little too fat.

And now utter despair as hair grows everywhere,
except on your head, though it once flourished there.
Waste disposal these days, a problem becomes,
you've no teeth anymore but a great set of gums.

Everything's winding down, though we don't seem to
mind,
Our desires have abated, our children are kind.
And they'd better be too, we'll be first in God's court,
they won't want us to turn in a lousy report.

Come with Me, My Love

September 20, 2012

Come with me, my love,
and we'll wander above
the North Bluff road on the hill.
Then down we'll go to the sea below,
to park and gaze on the view until
late afternoon sunbeams brightly fill
the ocean's expansive flow.

I'll look at you and you'll look at me,
by the look on your face I'll know,
to Kahuna's Fish and Chips
down by the sea,
I must surely quickly go.
For it's time to eat
as I hear repeat
of dinner bell's hello.

Then you and I together will sit
in the car's front seat
with horizon lit
by the setting sun
and we'll savor it
as we picnic on the go.

Where, oh so neat and orderly,
you'll pass my fish and chips to me.
I'll use ketchup and you will not,
and we'll marvel at all the fish we've got,
then devour it hungrily.
We'll clean up the mess with a pensive sigh,
we'll exchange a kiss then, you and I,
and back to Surrey we'll go.

This Day

January 5, 2013

This day
Is but another day
One more day
On the shelf
But is this day
In any way
Unique within itself

Or is it perhaps
As one might say
Anonymously plain
Not in the least
Distinguished, just
Another day
Again

But thinkest thou
How precious
Another day alive
Alternatively
One might say
At least
Thou didst survive

And even more
Importantly
Thou hast not
Gone to hell
Christ yet awaits
At heaven's gates
As far as I can tell

Creation Sound

October 31, 2011

Since light as it travels
is faster than sound,
and starlight's
been around
since creation,
when creation occurred
a loud noise would abound,
to regale us with
great expectation?

You'd think that by now
we'd be hearing the sound
as it happened way back
when the heavens erupt.
That crashing and banging
would have been profound,
from the time all the parts
of creation blew up.

Though intelligent reasoning
would seem to negate
such wild exaggeration.
My intellect clear
simply cannot relate
as I wait in anticipation.

I must yet understand
and must try not to fret,
but how come
we ain't heard
from creation yet?

Cricket's Song

August 10, 2012

Somewhere deep in the grass nearby,
I hear the cheep of a cricket's cry.
God would know what he's trying to say,
as through the evening he cheeps away,
he can only try.

Perhaps it's a love song, a girl to win,
as he sings all night to entice her in.
Perhaps she'll demure coquettishly,
and want to be sure he'll faithful be,
as the night goes by.

It might be that he doesn't have much time,
a lifespan of hours by God's design.
This gives a new slant to his urgency,
to find a lady in time before he,
must bid good-bye

But there is one thing I would like to know,
when winter comes, where do crickets go.
For nary a peep do I hear from them,
for a whole twelve months of the year and then,
they drop by again.

Does a cricket resort exist down below,
for them to escape the ice and snow.
Where they revel and holiday most of the year,
then when cricket time again comes near,
they reappear.

Whatever the answer, I think it's neat,
in the heat of the summer to hear them cheep.
Reassuring us all, life does go on,
evidenced again by the cricket's song,
repeat, repeat, repeat.

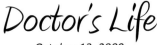

Doctor's Life

October 13, 2009

Our doctor friends
their work portends
that they must go
where brave men fear to tread.

Devoted life to meet these ends
their destiny of course intends
they probe in places
mortal man would dread.

Daily they enquire into
secrets kept from me, and you
must discretely follow through,
not limited to just the patient's head.

Good taste requires we not name names
of places patients suffer pains;
these places doctor entrance gains
requiring we lie prostrate on his bed.

Scanty gown with just a tie
dignity has said good-bye
baring all as there we lie
seen it all before, the Nursey said.

Doctor, totally nonplussed as
blithely he examines us;
we've given him our total trust
the panic in our eyes he's surely read.

Paid him with the usual fee
felt he should be paying me
for letting him my secrets see
embarrassed, I was wishing I was dead.

Nursey wipes my sweating brow
never mind, it's over now
managed to survive somehow
sauntered to the door...discretely fled.

Does Size Matter?

October 30, 2010

In medieval England fair,
one finds jousting everywhere.
Emerging now from grand abode,
onto field of valor rode,
on giant charger, valiant knight,
prancing, looking for a fight.

When down the field at other end,
our miniature equestrian friend,
on pony hardly four feet tall,
feet barely clearing ground at all,
came charging on with manner bold,
eliciting great mirth, we're told.

Reigned in pony with a snort,
though much too tiny for this sport,
forsooth, *en garde,* sir, this is it,
forsooth yourself, you silly twit,
bold knight replied with great chagrin,
refusing to acknowledge him.

Our midget, slamming face plate shut
commenced to charge opponent, but
opponent chose to not engage.
Our midget then with great enrage,

tickled under stallion's flank,
who then let wind and really stank.

When valiant knight, entrapped within
his suit of armor made of tin,
grew languid from the gas attack,
fell off charger on his back.

He landed with enormous clatter,
midget said it didn't matter,
threw his little midget mace
directly at opponent's face.
Just like David slew the giant,
our midget slew bold knight defiant.

Endless Creation

September 8, 2011

As mortal men, in wonderment and awe,
upon the mounts of heaven gaze,
with eyes that cross and sometimes glaze,
how little we yet know.

Technology, the way for modern man
to build his Babel right to heaven's gates.
Where God is mocked, what destiny awaits
as man's rebellion seems to ever grow.

Admittedly, man's instruments might know,
not the storied ancient one of days,
but farthest, faintest, slightest hint of haze
that instruments of man could ever show.

Astronomers inform us that the light we see
from twinkling star is merely ancient history
from eons far, to we who are
adrift in endless space down here below.

And so, what is there beyond the stars now seen,
what lies beyond that far impenetrable screen?
For surely mortal man has never been
a witness to that vast creation glow.

A man I'm told, could travel at the speed of light
for all his life, say eighty years, each day and night,
and never would his interplanetary travels flow
beyond the heavens God created long ago.

And anyway, his travels could not terminate, my friend,
that suggestion predicates infinity must end.
So if you end infinity, then where, O where,
is that somewhere, away out there,
with all his wisdom, modern man's intrepid scan,
might go.

Exuberant Mental Sagacity

September 20, 2012

Some seemingly have the capacity
for exuberant mental sagacity,
which is plain to see
for they seem to be
forever, very evidently,
engaged quite deeply in thought.

They rarely open their mouth to speak,
preferring to quietly sit and seek
as far as anyone can tell,
and they do this very, very well,
deep things of life as they ought.

People seeking their sage advice
will humbly sit at their feet.
They pontificate
as though they know,
the answer to questions
seekers will throw,
but their answer is usually
yes or no,
I'm surprised they've never been caught.

So don't confuse that age-old ruse
of quietly refusing to speak.

They seem quite wise, but I realise
they're pulling a bluff, it's just a disguise.
If you're really seeking, the place to go
when you really, really need to know,
is here at my feet for advice.

Down Memory Lane

October 16, 2010

I can't remember why we do it,
but we seldom get right to it,
for I'm certain
we will never have success.
It just seems the thing to do
when we're together, me and you,
a latent instinct irrepressible, I guess.

Now the consequence of hunger
in our lives when we were younger,
was to quickly fill that need,
our hunger sate.
However, now that we're much older,
body temperature much colder,
dozing off does nothing
to ingratiate.

We're no longer multiplying,
I vaguely do remember trying,
they say the world is populating
much too fast.
I guess it really is a blessing,
Seniors constantly digressing,
we might have known
that it was much too good to last.

Exercise

October 30, 2010

It seems like only yesterday,
we'd walk to keep the fat away,
we always used to take a hike,
or maybe even ride a bike.
Then everybody got a car,
now no one's walking very far,
we're getting fat and don't like that,
So Exercise, Oh Exercise,
the modern holy grail.

All day we're very sedentary,
piling on the fat.
Remote controls they say are great,
to get up now I really hate,
my vacuum is remote controlled,
I sit admiring how it rolled,
my belly's growing, fold on fold,
it used to be so flat.
So Exercise, Oh Exercise,
that must be where it's at.

Now walking can be dangerous,
I heard somebody say,
their grandpa started walking
at least five miles every day.

Grandpa with their grandma,
never seemed to get on right,
he started walking yesterday,
they saw him leave last night.
So Exercise, Oh Exercise,
he walked right out of sight.

The only time for exercise
is really very early,
before you open up your eyes,
and life starts getting surly.
You will be glad you lost the flab,
that exercise you took,
for when you die you'll realize why,
reclining you forsook.
Because of all that Exercise,
they'll say how good you look.

Father Time

December 5, 2012

When father time
On task divine
Arrives to take me out
On that last day
To steal away
On my last walkabout
I'll keep a sharp eye
Peeled for him
And when he knocks
I'll let him in
The front door
I'll go out the back
While he politely waits
I'll pull that little
Sneak attack
That surely irritates
He'll leave with all
His dander up
When he returns
To pick me up
I've changed my name
Then he'll refrain
From coming here
For me again

He'll go about
His daily round
And I'll just slip his mind
Freedom for me
Will then abound
I know I never will be found
At least till dinnertime

Food Factory

May 31, 2011

Life, ah life,
ceaselessly pulsing unseen.
As we look at a growing
tomato or pepper,
a leafy green plant
that's producing whatever,
it motionless seems,
and just grows automatic,
but that plant to which
we're relating as static,
if we ever would pause
to ponder and dream,
we'd discover is moving,
or so it would seem.

Could we ever endeavour
to venture inside
that leafy green stem,
we would go for a ride
on a river of magical
nutritive juices,
surging through channels
and courses and sluices,
from the root's furthest depth,
on an elegant trip,

as we elevate up to the highest tip,
where nature's machinery
of food reproduction,
impels us through elegant
greenery's induction,
to the uppermost
wonderful gift from God. Delicious creation
we stand to applaud,
A GREEN BEAN!

Forever and a Day

August 24, 2012

Some eighty-seven years have passed,
so filled with memories.
Embellished over time so vast,
so many souls and mysteries
replay.

Upon the frames within my head,
they pass before me, one by one.
Those endless memories are read
from back before time ever was
displayed.

What trick is this that memories play,
with countenance so vital.
Are they not living then within
my memory bank to yet begin
again today?

They were so vital, oh so young,
I roll them out in vast array.
Did they grow old and then become
like me so fraught with living's numb
decay?

This cannot be, I knew them well,
so full of life's vitality.
Though I grow old, they still must dwell
in life's adventures they might tell
to me some day.

So till that day I'll ever strive
within my memories so clear.
To keep each one of them alive,
then all together we'll survive
forever and a day.

Here's to the Bee

October 14, 2011

A thing of beauty
Sweet flower petal
Bursts into the world
A platform to settle
For hungry bee
To make honey for me
If no flower existed
My tongue sadly twisted
Like vinegar sour
For bee cannot scour
The meadow for pollen
My demeanour fallen
My chin on the ground
If no honey is found
So here's to the petal
And here's to the bee
And here's to the pollen
Bees gather for free
And here's to the honey
And here's to the hive
And here's to the flowers
That keep us alive

And here's to the rest
They all take in the Fall
But here is to God
The designer of all.

Hip Pip Hurray

October 29, 2011

Must be alive
I plainly see
For if they
Cut an artery
Or any other
Part of me
I bleed

And if I bleed
Without restraint
There's not
The slightest doubt
There ain't
That I might die
Or maybe I
Might lucky be
And only faint

But if I die
I do suspect
My pension
I cannot collect
Won't need
A pension anyway

Couldn't spend it
On the way
To that Hallelujah day
I resurrect
Hip Pip Hooray!

I Really Must Go

November 29, 2012

Whene'er we meet
On uneasy street
You say, how do you do
I then proceed
With utmost speed
To share with you
My every need
Responding to your cue

You quickly interject
And doff
Your hat to say,
I must be off
Before another word I say
You've disappeared
You've gone away

I know you must
Desire to know
Extent of
My vicissitudes
To paper now
My pen must go
Missives sent
Will overflow

With sorrows
That your tender ear
Will cause to weep
The day you hear
The tale you missed
The day you had
To disappear
But never fear
I'll let you know

Idiosyncratic Ambiguity

September 28, 2010

Big words, idiosyncratic ambiguity, explain a situation
when
a spoken word or something writ, you have to check
again.
For that something writ or spoken can have meanings,
more than one,
Now, some idiosyncratic examples, pay attention
everyone.

If a deaf child signs bad swear words, do they wash his
hands with soap.
Would a fly that hasn't any wings, be called a walk...I
hope.

Could there possibly in English be, another word for
synonym,
or if no hypothetical questions, then how would one
beginonym?

If we asked a clerk to show us to the store's self-help
section,
Would it defeat the purpose, if she whispered the
direction?

If one with multi-personalities says, himself he plans to kill,
is this a hostage situation, forced against the other's will?

If an animal endangered, eats a plant endangered too,
which one has priority, whatever must you do?

Could a vegetarian person, animal crackers eat,
or if a Civil War was civil, now wouldn't that be neat?

If you try real hard to fail, and you finally succeed,
is that failure or success, an explanation now I need?

Amongst swimmers synchronized, I really wish I knew,
if one swimmer sadly drowned, would the rest drown too?

Can an atheist get insurance, against those acts of God so called,
and where do Forest Rangers go to "get away from it all"?

If police arrest a Mime, is remaining silent still his right,
if you ate pasta and antipasto, you'd then still be hungry, right?

What was the best thing, before they invented sliced bread?
One nice thing about egotists, they won't talk about others, enough said.

And how do they train the deer to cross the highway, day or night,
at those lovely yellow road signs where the crossing is their right?

And don't you think it's cruel to those with speech impediment,
to put an "S" in the word lisp, now what was their intent?

Please don't sweat the petty things, and never pet the sweaty things.
If man evolved from apes and monkeys, why do we still have apes and monkeys?

If a turtle is without his shell, however, ever could we tell,
if our poor friend lives homelessly, or is it naked he must be?

Bathrooms in gas stations, well locked they always seem,
are they afraid someone will come, the dirty mess to clean?

Why ever on sour cream, is there a date of expiration,
old or new, it's certain to provide that sour sensation?

If a person Oriental, is spun around three times,
is he then disoriented, or just in oriental climes?

Atheists when organized, reject God with great elation,
which is sad, for now they had, a non-prophet
organization.

All these thoughts come from other folk, if I could that
clever be,
I'd be some famous genius, not just simple, little old
me.
But this silliness is lots of fun, we've had a happy time,
my part was to reorganize and try to make them
rhyme.

Inheritance

July21, 2011

Just as I was in
my father
and my father
was in his.
Would it have
been a bother
to put me in
a richer father,
I would certainly
much rather,
you know how it is.

'Twould be lovely
to inherit,
to be rich
above the throng.
And you know
of course I'd share it,
but I'll have to
grin and bear it,
wealth they say
can't make you happy,
I would love
to prove them wrong.

Inside Surprise
November 10, 2011

Did you ever endeavour to venture inside
To gaze into that maw, your big mouth open wide
Well one time I looked deep into my gaping maw
And you'll never believe all the stuff that I saw
There were levels extreme, your indulgence I beg
Reaching down it would seem, to my hollow leg
With wee tiny workers all rushing around
Seeking elements needed that had to be found
I heard one little fella, cry loudly for chrome
To stop the hair loss on the top of my dome
While another sends helium up level three
They detected a hole in my chest cavity
That leak could deplete all my gravity
Then I saw a whole crowd, in my belly I think
All with one voice, they were crying for zinc
For the smell you could tell, was a cryin' disgrace
They were slippin' and slidin' all over the place
Then one little fella sent up sasparella
To deal with my belly fat
They used the whole tub when they started to rub
But my belly they couldn't make flat
Then I saw a whole crew heading south to my shoe
With spoonfuls of selenium
They were rushing down there to get rid of the hair
For a jungle my legs had become

I then saw with dismay at the end of the day
Their energy start to deplete
I heard some of them say if I'd just hit the hay
They could all get a little sleep
So I pulled back my head and jumped into my bed
And listened with all of my might
I'm sure now I know, they're asleep down below
Cause I heard them all saying good night

Inspiration

October 8, 2011

What can I say
Muse left today
On feathery feet
Down the golden way
To the heart of another
Whose labours sway
All through the night
To break of day
Her agony reaching
Forth from night
When the Muse arrives
Mounting into the light
Of elegant rhyming
That bursts from the heart
Of the lover subliming
Revealing her part
As thoughts tumble out
As excitements mount
As the verbiage flows
As the hours count
And the twilight falls
At the end of day
And the muse departs
And the thoughts go away
To where I await

The Muse's return
In my emptiness
Holding a heartfelt yearn
For inspiration
To agitate
The flow of ideas
My mind to inflate
Hooray she's come
The Muse is here
Out the window
Eject my fear
As happy again
Amidst mounting flame
I write, I write, I write.

Intrepid Hunter, I

August 24, 2011

I bought a gun, a little gun,
to hunt a little Deer.
Went to the woods the other day,
where little Deer all live and play,
and though I tried in every way,
the Deer would not come near.

I scratched my head and wondered why,
then overheard one little guy
exhibiting no fear.
To his friend begin to tell,
why all the Deer were laughing,
and rolling on the ground with glee,
they knew exactly where I'd be,
my posterior telegraphing.

So, went into my small backyard,
and practiced, oh so very hard,
invisibility.
Then tried again, to no avail,
the ending to this sorry tale,
I visit now the butcher store,
and don't go hunting anymore,
or practice in my backyard for,
neighbours were photographing.

It Rained Today

December 1, 2012

It rained today
But then in winter
On this coast
We get the most
The rain is truly
Here to stay
From Thanksgiving
At least till May
It comes
And will not go away
But then for me
That's quite okay
It guarantees
A nice display
Of posies
In my garden gay
Upon the merry
Month of May
Hooray!
Hooray!
Hooray!

Just a-Kickin' the Can

October 20, 2012

Well, I've made it this far,
at the end of the day.
Though the sun's shinin' still,
I'm not makin' much hay.

But I guess that's all right,
for as old as I am.
I'm just travelin' along,
just a-kickin' the can.

And it's good to sit back,
give the young guys a chance.
These old legs hangin' slack,
are too old for the dance.

Oh! The spirit's still willin',
but the flesh is too weak.
I could use penicillin,
right now as I speak.

But it's good to reflect
on the glories long past.
All the years I collect,
are retiring at last.

Now a word to the wise,
as I leave this old earth.
Settle stakes with Lord Jesus,
give slew foot a wide berth.

Just Ordinary Guys

October 4, 2012

Who makes these stupid rules,
why spik and nipper, kraut and kike?
They're playing us for fools,
why can't men, each other like?

To keep us at each other's throats,
fulfills some hidden plan.
Some party hack expounds, emotes,
against his fellow man.

Then nation against nation,
demonizes all of them.
They're hateful, cruel, each one a fool,
not even really men.

They say it's propaganda,
that it helps to win the war,
In any tongue, caramba,
that's what propaganda's for.

But then the war is ended,
and we find to our surprise,
after fighting is suspended,
they're just ordinary guys.

Now, I recognise with great remorse,
sometime we have to fight.
We surely must defend, of course,
determine wrong from right.

But the problem's not us little fry's,
it's the leaders, we assume.
Exchange our leaders, big surprise,
one year to rule the other guys,
they'd sing a different tune.

Lady-Killer

September 3, 2011

While a ladybug was walking
down a flower stem one day.
bumped into a caterpillar,
looking quite the lady killer,
who was bound the other way.

The caterpillar looked the same
when viewed from either end.
So ladybug could never know,
which direction he would go,
or what he would intend.

Now caterpillar was renowned
in meadow far and wide.
As a charming lady-killer,
known in fact as killer-diller,
and was looking for a bride.

Now, since he was getting older,
degradation was profound.
But no one had ever told her,
in the eye of the beholder,
is where beauty will be found.

Ladybug was feeling mellow, as she
cuddled by his side.
He was quite the handsome fellow,
with his stripes of black and yellow,
as her insides turned to Jell-O,
she became his blushing bride.

Let's Give God a High Five

March 19, 2012

Beware, take care,
this aught'a give you a scare.
One day you'll discover
from Father and Mother,
whose genes that day got together to play,
resulting in little old you or your brother,
or even a sister from clay
they say,
yes, even a sister from clay.

For the elements wild that go into a child
all come from the earth,
so that all they are worth, is a bucket of dust
mixed together with water,
and if that does not
bring you alarm as it aughter,
your perception exhibits a dearth
or worse,
you could even be thought perverse.

Until God breathed in the spirit of life
you were only a lump of clay.
This revelation fills me with delight,
so I holler hooray with all my might.
Your spirit came at the start of the game,

each spirit arrived, not by Mother contrived,
until it invaded, nothing paraded,
to indicate you were alive, alive.
So let's give God a high five,
okay?
Let's give God a high five.

Let's Make Rhyming the Law
September 15, 2012

Why does modern poetry sound so inane,
confusing us in its expression?
The art of the poet, obliquely arcane,
this attempt to be artsy, again and again,
like a school girl's romantic confession.

Why must the poet with eloquence, wax,
what's wrong with that old word, become.
Why does its obtuseness consistently tax
ones old-fashioned longing for simple syntax,
leaving restful enjoyment unstrung.

When describing the stars or romancing in cars,
must two hearts be entwined into one.
Must the cherry tree blossoms be snow on the ground,
not just nature's off scouring where fruit will be found
after plenty of water and sun.

So the true remedy, quite apparent to me,
let's not call a round shovel, a spade.
A spade is a spade, if my point might be made,
let's put an end to this pompous charade,
let's make rhyming the law, by decree.

Life's Passions

January, 31, 2010

I'm not the man I used to be,
divested passions, one by one.
Food remaining now, for me,
to dinner bell, respond with glee,
since single life begun.

That preoccupied short order cook,
had better pay attention.
He's messing with the single thing
remaining, to fulfillment bring,
from all of life's invention.

Since conjugal love has fled my coop,
no longer to reside.
One thing alone will constitute,
there is no other substitute,
than lovely breaded chicken,
southern fried.

Limbo

April 29, 2012

Limbo, a place neither here nor there,
no one attends if they have any sense.
It lies they tell me, not anywhere,
as one might imagine, of consequence.
For it cannot it seems, be easily contained,
with borders quite indefinable.
If you come with intentionality aimed,
and your curiosity unrestrained,
you will find it irreconcilable.
You are not departing,
yet have not arrived,
with courage that's smarting
and pride contrived,
you have a beginning,
but never an end,
you dream of winning
but never contend.
You're trapped in limbo,
entreated to stay,
just cut your losses
and break away.
You can't explain
you don't know why,
you'll suffocate here
till the day you die.

You'll know that limbo's
a deadly trap,
but you'll never find it
on any map.
Kick over the traces,
the only way
you'll ever accomplish
a meaningful day,
or so folks say.

Long-Necked Friends

October 20, 2011

What's in a name
Or in my name
At any rate
Shall I be known
Might fame suffice
My name recall
Beyond this life
Where I'm not known
At all
What worldly epitaph
Might then relate

Might there even be
Some merit to extol
As days
They dwindle down
To just a few
I've searched in vain
To find an honour roll
Alas, a search
Quite fruitless in review

But with this thought
Sweet comfort
Now surround

Reflecting on
The wonderful
And long-necked
Friends I've found
We all are clothed
With joy
May I remind
Our heads
Are all in heaven
While our feet
Are on the ground

Lost Cause

November 12, 2012

I know my hair is thinning
As it slowly fades away
This alas, is the beginning
Of a battle void of winning
I can see the mirror grinning
As I brush it every day

I suppose it is in keeping
With the gradual betray
Of my muscle mass depleting
And each orifice secreting
An involuntary reeking
Indicating great decay

Where I used to leap each railing
I now grovel underneath
When we walk I'm always trailing
My older friend ahead, regaling
All the girls so hearty, haling
While I'm panting for relief

I do try to be a winner
And I will before I die
I'll work hard at being thinner
Try to eat a smaller dinner

Though I am just a beginner
Yes, another piece of pie

Lost Yesterdays

November 17, 2012

Twilight at last, the day scarce past
Sun blazing o'er horizon yet
Till tranquilly, our sun doth set
Whilst with us yet, 'tis still today For
those out west, 'tis yesterday The
sun o'er them is shining still They'll
not have our today until
The sun doth kiss our world good-bye
And darkness filleth all their sky
Then, while we still possess our day
Back to the east, tomorrow lay
Not our tomorrow, no not yet
They see sun first, let's not forget
But if we carry this too far
We'll be confusing where we are
For over on the world's far side
Doth yesterday yet still abide
Or hath tomorrow then arrived
If man doth travel with yon sun
Could new day ever have begun
Oh! Unsolvable conundrum

Lovely Rain

November 13, 2010

Ah! Rain, sweet rain
has come again
to trickle down the windowpane.
Glistening great, bright, shiny drops.
Into the night it never stops,
to wipe away is vain.

For I know, my friend,
of your heart's contend
with summer's warm untimely end.
Emptying out from heaven's vaults,
rain arrives, bright sun defaults,
just as the gods intend.

For rain, we know
on the fields below,
lubricates the crops we grow.
We'd miss those salads and stringy peas
if you had your way, so I decrees,
a nightly dose of H20.

Cheer up, we locals freely boast,
that most of the year on the western coast
the sun keeps residents warm as toast.
Occasional rain, falls only at night,

in early morning at dawn's first light,
the sun arrives for it's daily roast.

To explain, summer rain only at night
was made the law by plebiscite.
I can hear you shouting, "That can't be right,"
as you jump up and down on your Sunday hat,
'cause the rain must rain, for all o' that.
But you'll never know, try as hard as you might,
this secret ordained for our delight.

Male Prostate

September 10, 2012

The male prostate with age
doth diminish.
Then what's left at the end,
without any pretend,
the Doc will quite casually finish.

His rude finger excludes
anesthetic.
While demeanor exudes,
what could be misconstrued,
as detachment sublimely aesthetic.

The cure requires chemical castration,
a relatively painless event.
A gradual reduction,
of what once meant seduction,
and we don't even know where it went.

Do not be apprehensive my friend,
you won't realize what you miss.
At our age it's endemic,
becomes quite academic,
and reduced to exclusively p--s.

Metamorphosis

November 20, 2010

Come visit, lovely flying flower,
briefly grace our garden bower.
Blithe butterfly we only borrow,
here today, gone tomorrow.

Was not ever quite so flightful,
former terra firma bite full,
candidate for bird beak killer,
tasty, crawling caterpillar.

I wonder, would his mem'ry bring
remembrance, how he learned to cling,
when through leafy jungle crawl,
caring not that he might fall?

This munchy caterpillar age
devouring garden's foliage
prepares him for life's destiny,
airborning acrobatically.

Could he know that one day soon,
he'd spin himself a silk cocoon?
From sleepy metamorphosis
to carefree butterflying bliss.

Rhapsodizing bloom to bloom,
transporting pollen, very soon
depositing where're he stops,
guaranteeing next year's crops.

Existence is, most probably
assured by nature so that he
continues on to propagate
our garden's grand, a lovely fate.

Midnight Capers
December 4, 2010

"It's time to go to bed my dear,"
these words most evenings around here,
whenever news is over, I impart.
By then we're ready to retire,
to sleep, our imminent desire,
so either wife or I will make a start.

On this night in particular,
she left it rather late for her,
retiring after I was fast asleep.
This tale so far sounds quite mundane,
but later you'll be glad you came,
to hear the date with destiny we keep.

As I'm dreaming very peacefully,
you know how silly dreams can be,
I dreamt that I was driving star to star.
I was rammed by this big rocket ship,
on an inter-planetary trip,
which did a lot of damage to my car.

The collision reverberated loud,
and tossed my wife out on a cloud,
I had no idea where she went.
I sat bolt upright in the night,

and hurriedly turned on the light,
to see if she'd survived the big event.

Midnight Terror

August 7, 2012

As we walk in the night on a lonely road,
looking over our shoulder as terrors forebode.
The shadows cast by the full moon's light
seem to move on their own, eliciting fright,
as onward with quickening step we strode.

Stop this foolishness, we ourselves reprimand,
as a shadow moved in the shape of a hand.
With a branch in the gloom looking just like a rope,
while down at its end hung what looked like a throat,
and our breathing we haste to expand.

Though the night is chill, we're clammy and wet,
as we're shaking and trying, our fear to forget.
All the spirits of fear are abroad in the night
as the devil is licking his chops with delight,
I'd be willing to bet.

Hark now, be still, did you hear that sound,
no, I must be mistaken, there's no one around. But
there must be, there is, I just heard it again.
There's no other pursuer that I can explain,
after me as I'm homeward bound.

I saw somebody move at the branch in the road,
A little ahead, just before our abode.
Lord, what can I do, is he lying in wait
to eat me alive at my garden gate.
Oh Father! Dear Father, you gave me a fright!
I should not walk alone at this time of night!

Morning Song

April 30, 2011

A Robin's morning conversation,
heralding the break of dawn.
Snowy head at rest beside me,
deaf to cheery Robin's song.

Happy sound of life above me,
symphony of world's awake.
Stirring, sunning, showers running,
smell of kitchen's breakfast make.

Moving through the morning hustling,
doors that open, doors that slam.
Sliced bread serving, Mother shuffling,
dealing hungry toast and jam.

Down the staircase tumble, flowing,
car doors slam as motors roar.
We snuggle under blankets knowing,
silence soaring, like before.

Ah! The peace that now pervading,
inundates our cozy room.
Robin's music serenading
seniors wakened much too soon.

Mountains of Cumulus

May 1, 2012

How majestically, mountains of cumulus pile,
to gallantly roll through the sky.
Framed in gorgeous blue just to dazzle you
with pile upon pile to bewitch and beguile,
full sailed galleons with banners high.

Then later the clouds take a threatening look
as the galleons, their cannons explode.
The bright flashes of light are a frightening sight,
the thunder of cannon erupts in the night
while the heavenly lightning glowed.

Now the heavens do battle, the rains tumble down,
a deluge of flood through the night.
These cascades releasing on ocean and plain
in torrents engulfing, this ravaging rain
is impossible really, to fight.

This great volume of water, we can't comprehend,
must be a huge ocean all right.
How can it suspend in the cloud mass this way, to
blithely stay dry in the heavens all day,
and then empty the heavens at night?

This mystery simple, I cannot explain,
meteorology's not in my line.
But I hope you'll agree it's a great mystery,
so if we ever meet, please explain it to me.
Is it simply all God's grand design?

My Name

October 8, 2011

My name,
the one bequeathed at birth,
unheralded through life.
Though a threadbare worn,
unheard, forlorn,
identifying device.
It will fulfill my needs until
I exit earthly strife,
and not just me, it will you see,
do likewise for my wife.

What's in a name,
the poet asked,
perhaps with tongue in cheek.
A rose by any other name
would surely smell as sweet.
And that's the point I make,
you see,
if on other name rely,
it could not change
the truth that he,
most certainly am I.

My name,
it will be cast adrift
when I'm no longer here,
I hope it's not forgotten,
but some other frame endear.
I hope he does it justice
and adopts my name with pride,
but not as a famous poet,
this I never could abide.
For then I'd be diminished,
he would overshadow me,
write better poetry than I,
most surely you can see,
for one so modest, as am I,
this must not ever be.

Name Change

October 23, 2012

This day
That's called today
Today
Must find life
Full of sorrow
Tomorrow
He's called
Yesterday
And yesterday,
Tomorrow

NANO NANO

October 30, 2011

There's a "Nano" level of life in us all,
a hidden cellular exchange.
Our billions of cells must interrelate,
almost instantly, leaving no time to wait,
cells constantly rearrange.

In the blink of an eye, cells multiply,
specific to every need.
Some cells are born while other cells die,
it's all God's design, they don't have to try,
and it happens with breathtaking speed.

Such intricate, fabulous, complex design,
just boggles my simple mind.
How do they know when it's time to split,
or others to cash in their chips and quit,
and how do they know which kind?

To create human life is a dream of man,
in his medical labs to strive.
But God must inject man's spirit and soul,
else a body is lifeless, can never be whole,
God says, I kill and I make alive.

No Substance

September 6, 2012

Letter to the editor
See my name in print
But hardly any credit for
My name on the interior
So small I have to squint

Yesteryear 'twas all the rage
Public's opinion to engage
On editorialist page
With socialistic tint
To lather up the populace
For politicians in the race
Vying, but in every case
No substance, only lint

Newspapers now
Have gone the way
Of Dodo bird
Or Hemingway
What took their place
To fill the day
Let me give you a hint

Talking heads
On television
Short delay
Means no revision
Everything is
Peppermint
All agree
Without incision
Greeted now
With great derision
Wonder where
Man's honour went

Obfuscation

October 23, 2012

What would I do
If I were you
And you were me
Today
This can't be true
I can't be you
Your feet are made of clay

And furthermore
You can't be me
Because you see
In me
There'd never be
Quite room enough
You weigh
Two thirty-three

Perhaps we'd best
Just stay the same
The way
We were designed
Because the folks
We know the most
Would think
They're going blind

Obsolescence

April 21, 2012

And now the years so swiftly flown,
a weary burden do impart
to one who latterly has shown
ineptitude from weakness grown
as vestiges of strength depart.

Alas, the casual mind commands
the legs to move in such a way.
But rank rebellion now begins,
no movement from defiant limbs,
to puzzled will's dismay.

So patience now is forced upon
possessor of commanding brain.
The brain says move, an empty song,
coordination now is gone,
but where might one complain?

The brain says go, the legs say wait,
imposed upon one's will.
To stand immobile seems one's fate,
embarrassed when arriving late,
another bitter pill.

But never mind, one must resign
oneself to nature's sway.
There is one problem though for me,
demanding utmost urgency,
why ever must the bathroom be
an hour's walk away?

Ode to Agnes Mary

November 30, 2012

At eves descent, come 'way with me
To walk the shore unseen
Enraptured by the ocean's
roar Two hearts as one
between
I'll be your handsome troubadour
And you, my English queen

The gulls' betimes, soft flutter down
To ocean's open grave
To raft on billowy eiderdown
As froth on gentle wave
Indifferent to my queen's renown
Or pleasure that she gave

Again then, boldly pledge my troth
Eternally to thee
I see the gods in heaven wroth
Wouldst I but disagree
Or cause my queen to suffer loss
Oh! Woe betideth me

Ode to Chicken Soup

November 17, 2012

What alchemy dost thou invoke
In this thy ancient kitchen brew
Where, seemingly with genius stroke
Life's passion all within, awoke
To homage pay to you

What sumptuousness dost thou bring
From ordinary, common thing
Such culinary aptitude
Doth blendest them together now
In honeymoon, and then somehow
To sacrificially exude
Bouquet that maketh kitchen sing

Chicken pieces, leave the skin
Resides there, extra taste within
Just strain the broth at later date
Leaves clarity to then relate
A carrot, mayhap one or two
And lentils, just a generous few
Some onions, pungent, magical
Tart kings of things botanical

Some celery, so crisp and sweet
Most secretly thou dost entreat
Flavoured now with heart of love
Simmering to God above
Voila! Chicken Soup!

Old-Age Travel
July 31, 2011

I once traveled far by plane and car,
in the rosy days of youth.
Those halcyon times would fare with thee,
expending my days so carelessly,
while trifling with the truth.

But the utter restraint,
by age made faint,
that tethers me now to a chair.
In truth brings release,
where all boundaries cease,
as my mind soars through the air.

I now visit the Riviera gay,
in my yacht of splendid design,
or drop in on Rome,
when my mind leaves home,
in my jet at dinner time.

Maybe visit a sunny southern isle,
whenever the fancy moves,
I can come and go,
either fast or slow,
not caring if one approves.

But the wonderful part,
that touches my heart,
and my pocketbook sublime,
is the airline fee,
because now, you see,
it doesn't cost me a dime.

Old Bones

November 8, 2011

I knew them then and I knew them well,
one from the other, could easily tell.
Old friends in life through years flown by,
but I see them now with an inward eye.

For they all have left as time passed by,
one by one unexpectedly.
To know them now could I even try,
if their bones came together erectedly.

I'm afraid they would all look quite the same,
one from the other I'd never tell.
When the poet emoted, what's in a name,
this could now apply to dead friends, as well.

What good would it do if I recognized,
or perhaps more likely, if they knew me?
I'd become I'm sure, quite exercised,
from talking bones, I would madly flee.

What a mental picture that thought bestows,
with skeletons chasing me, bones a-rattle.
As my hair and nightshirt behind me flows,
and I wake in a sweat from this nightmare battle.

So farewell, old friends, may you rest in peace,
my perambulations at night must cease.
Each other we knew when our bones were clad,
let's just leave it that way, then we'll all be glad.

Our "Down" Is Their "Up"

September 17, 2011

"Down" is a place I'm now able to see,
exists in the universe, relative to me.
Now as far as the rest of you folks are concerned,
you must find your own, as it must be discerned.

For "down" you must know, is not always down,
as the astronauts found when they shot out of town.
They found that their "down" didn't join them in
space,
for there nothing falls "down," it falls up in your face.

Upside down, a position they cannot assume,
as they're floating through space in their tiny
bathroom.
This problem was solved with some kind of creation,
the details I'll leave to your imagination.

And if when you walk, you just happen to trip,
you won't have to worry, you won't need to grip
a handrail for safety, you'll just do a flip
and end up on the ceiling, which becomes your floor,
it's so easy, you cannot fall down anymore.

Your fall down, your get down, your sit down is gone,
till you come back to earth, which is where they
belong.
You then will recover your "down" back again,
then when you fall down, you'll again suffer pain.

But relative to China, your "down" is their "up,"
so how do they keep their green tea in the cup.
And relative to us, they all stand on their head,
so why don't those people fall down out of bed.

Pain Pill

June 6, 2011

I had a pain, I took a pill,
prescribed for me against my will.
I struggled hard, it had to be,
though pill seemed far too large to me.

Alas! Alack! Confounded pill,
affliction aggravating still.
Pill won't work, for now I see,
should be inserted rectally.

Please Rain Again

August, 2009

Heated July has come,
close in on everyone.
What can we do with it,
wish we were through with it?

Oh for the days
when inclemency favoured us.
Rain fell and cool weather's tenancy
neighboured us.

With no perspiration
deflation inhibits us.
Heat consternation
then no longer visits us.

Clouds in the sky
are a lovely delight for us.
We no longer decry
that they turn day to night for us.

Why were we praying
the sun to awake us?
Continually saying
the rain should forsake us.

Never again my
cracked lips complain.
Forever restrain
unkind quips about rain.

May the heavens be bountiful
fill me a fountain full.
Regale me for hours
with refreshing rain showers.

Poetic Mind

July 30, 2011

How fragile,
this poet's mind,
fleeing from despair.
Wistfully
will cast about,
first within
and then without, to
inspiration find.
After seeking all about,
defeat without
the slightest doubt,
there's nothing's left
to write about,
mind forever bare.

Then, out of nowhere
suddenly,
a thought kicks in
creatively.
Where it comes from
who can know,
he takes all the credit
though.

For after all
he is the one
who's talented,
this mother's son,
as anyone
with slightest
sensitivity
would know.
So be thee sensitive
and just agree
that it is so.

Poetic Urgency

August, 29, 2011

What is this urgency, what is this drive,
that persists in my gut, seems to eat me alive?
What is this tugging, this pulling my heart,
revealing a feeling that tears me apart?
Search me!

I'm not able to name it, nor ever contain it,
bear it no malice, nor endeavour to tame it.
At times creates pleasure, at other times pain,
and yet I'm submissive, again and again.
I really am!

I never did ask, it just simply arrived,
I don't call it up and it's never contrived.
It's sometimes creative, revealingly sweet,
so I polish, refine it to make it complete.
Voila!

And then I present it to some who might care,
though often they don't seem to know that it's there.
I feel that I'm casting my pearls before swine,
but that's not really true, at least most of the time.
Sometimes though!

When one's briefly accepted, I light up and grin,
but then back to obscurity, to my chagrin.
My work very soon, could be thought of as classic, but
then fade like the dinosaur era, Jurassic.
Ho Hum!

Poet's Conundrum

February 11, 2012

A starving artist
Surely smells
From hours of
Selfless passion
That's also what
A poet does
From hours of writing
Poems because
His only motivation was
Creating fashion

For if he took
The time to spend
On bodily ablution
His poetry
Would suffer loss
From disposition
Very cross
Degenerating
Gold to dross
Despicable solution

The only compromise
I see
To satiate diversion

Install a tub
For rub-a-dub
To sit all day
In water then
To waterproof
A pad and pen
For poet's
Grand immersion

Point of No Return
June 9, 2012

Nowadays as my essential self distills,
intensifying even while diminishing.
A thought once deemed electric
now just partially fulfills,
for thoughts electrifying
never pay electric bills,
without which,
I'd have difficulty finishing.

Having reached the point of no returning,
my destiny seems fated to proceed.
Things that once enthralled me
I no longer seem to need, the
destiny that called me, now is
picking up some speed, and
I'm racing downhill fast, my
bridges burning.

As I'm looking all about with trepidation,
frenzied mass activity I see.
A universal, unfulfillable condition
that will never bring redemption to fruition,
and this all-important factor seems to be.
A blind, voracious spending, never ending,
that ignores the plea that Jesus Christ is sending,

get off your narrow focus, follow me.

Now, myself I do not hold as an example
of a model Christian, holier than thou.
I am just a stinking sinner, as is every one of you,
hopelessly hell bound and I would likely be there now,
if Jesus had not saved me, and He'll surely save you
too,
if you'll just agree with God's decree,
submit to Jesus, follow me,
God's promises are true.

Potlicker

January 28, 2012

Do it now
Or even quicker
I am, I vow
A quick nitpicker
While beckoning
My old potlicker
Titus, my Great Dane

Enrolled him in
Obedience class
It's not a sin
Spent all my cash
We both completed
Head of class
And both respond now
In a flash
If he would just
Take out the trash
But I love him
Just the same

Property Rights

September 15, 2012

One problem for poets, if I might explain,
though we're idely, widely read.
Words swim in our bonnet, we try to get on it,
it's only a poem, we're not writing a sonnet,
as we're fighting, rejecting our bed.

Then the thought that appeared as our memory
cleared,
had relation to property rights.
All this space I command in, is mine to expand in,
you can't have this space, I require it to stand in,
though resistance precipitates fights.

You've got your own space, I exclaim to his face,
which you'd better regard with your life.
If you leave it I'll take it, you'd best not forsake it,
and watch where you're stepping, you're liable to
break it,
fool with me and you're entering strife.

And so daily it goes, my possessiveness shows,
but you really can't fault my desire.
Many millions stand waiting, to my space relating,
they could take it by stealthily appropriating,
it does make me afraid to retire.

But after all has been said, we must trot off to bed
and abandon our spaces until,
we awake in the a.m., primed, ready for mayhem,
then we all rush and dress, our own space to possess,
with uncertainty filling the bill.

But a brilliant solution came into my head,
that allows me to sleep every night.
An inflatable doll that I stand in the hall,
in the morning deflate him, and then imitate him,
repossessing my space, with no fight.

Queen Mary

October 27, 2010

When the stately Agnes Mary
like an ocean liner very
very regally, sedately settled
into Bobby's life, without
imposition slightest
and with touch the very lightest
she tied up to my berth
before I knew it, was my wife.

Married to my ocean liner
life could not have been sublimer
as she slowly moved about
without the slightest hint of speed,
like the mighty Ocean Mary
she would chart her course with very,
very little to belittle
very little to impede.

With our future looking cheery
resting oft, to not be weary
we both slowly stroll the strand
displaying Mary's English charm,
as we quaff the ocean air
we saunter on without a care
often seen together talking

while we're walking arm in arm.

Now this begins another life
with Queen Mary as my wife
together every day
we join in prayer.
It's so nice to sit together
in the house in stormy weather
what's the hurry,
we're not going anywhere.

Queen-Bed Led

October 6, 2009

White doddered head, reclining oft,
discreetly kissing pillow soft.
In bed surround, so snug and warm,
gently into slumber borne.

My queen displays, enticingly,
with greeting warm, invitingly.
Her blanket's lovely hugs surround,
as queen-sized sleep serenely found.

Languidly expectant lie,
on slumber's fantasies rely,
'twixt cotton cool to comfort me,
where dreams distort reality.

Early morn's invading chill
creeping over windowsill,
comforter from o'er my feet
cuddles up, with love discreet.

Snuggled in, just nose expose,
sleep the clock around, suppose,
embraced from face to toasty feet,
comfort undisturbed, replete.

And so, good night brigands, away,
with life's demands, I'm off to play,
in dreamland now, perchance withdraw,
to snore, more cords of wood to saw.

Rain-Pain

November 25, 2010

Snow is only rain, you know,
turned white from all the pain, you know,
descending to our nether region
where subzero temperature is legion,
a land of ice and snow.

Enveloped in a quiet shroud,
while living in their fluffy cloud,
unaware what fate awaits
while fluffy cloud still elevates,
high above the crowd.

But when it's time to rain again,
they're introduced to pain again.
Falling, twisting, screaming, hurting,
raindrops into snow converting,
useless to complain.

What next could this descent entail,
now transformed into stones of hail.
Doomed to go through freezing twice,
converted now to bouncing ice,
into destruction sail.

Though melting makes them disappear,
oblivion, they needn't fear,
while rain in Spain, song lyrics claim,
falls mainly in the soggy plain,
or so I hear.

The cycle flow they're following,
fills lakes from every little spring,
condensates up crystal clear,
back into clouds they hold so dear,
to rain again another year.

Renewal

September 15, 2011

Ah, life renewal, lends accrual
Please believe it dear
For if we did not have renewal
Nothing would be here

Renewal, necessary
Just as death must come, alas
The old must leave
To lend reprieve
For new to come to pass

This applies to you and me
And him and her and they
If you pay attention
You will notice the decay

Just think of all the fun you'll have
To help renewal come
So replicate yourselves en masse
Beginning, one on one

Satiety

November 23, 2012

I've surfeited on gollywogs
and indescribable limpets.
I far prefer each one to frogs,
which lay about in stinky bogs
and cuddle with frogettes.

After a feast of squirmy worms,
I always clean my plate.
I lap up all the tasty germs,
and laugh the way a plateful squirms
but never can escape.

Then afterward the waiter quoth,
dessert thou hast not tried.
At risk of sounding now, verbose

I gallantly replied,
sufficiency for now, I troth,
hath been suffonsified.

Say Not of Me

October 15, 2012

Say not of me
"Pretender to life's poetry"

Say otherwise
All insult that thou wilt

But never touch
This part of all in all
Of me

I shan't be here
But hopefully
Might linger free

Then surely as man's fall
Blood shalt be spilt

Scientifically Confusing

September 9, 2012

Men expound theoretical physics,
in a language obscenely obtuse.
While the physics I need,
must go through me with speed,
if for me they can be any use.

They expound on a theory called quantum,
having something to do with mechanics.
But that theory to me,
lacks relativity,
leaving little regard for its antics.

Men seem quite obdurate when inventfull,
with their magnets they play every day.
No one ever protests their credential,
as with reckless foray,
they desire to display,
their Magnetic Vector Potential.

But I know, to be smarter than me
must make them supremely, quite weory.
As they science away,
they most humbly display,
their Holonomic Atomic Brain Theory.

This will now terminate my preamble,
and I'm sure you'll agree, about time.
I don't know what amble this is pre to,
or the dis this might not agree to,
but you have to admire my design.

Silver Screen Fantasies

April 10, 2010

Please tell me, my friends, have you surmised
why the old-fashioned movies never survived.
Remember the cliffhanger feelings of dread till
our hero won out and the villain was dead.

And those wonderful, musical extravagances
where beautiful ladies all went through their dances
with impeccable timing and great syncopation
in multitudinous, colorful, costumed gyration.

And my friend Fred Astaire as he gracefully floated
through scene after scene, in my mind I promoted
myself to his place where our screen idol face
left the people in awe from our consummate grace.

And sweet Ginger Rogers, way up on that screen
poured her love out on me, and I felt really mean,
as reluctantly I must reject her advances,
with my sweetheart beside me, giving me glances.

Remember the wonderful feeling you got
from the dreamy, euphorically endearing plot
where the hero endures through each difficult time,
to end up with the girl while he banishes crime.

Our hearts would feel light at the end of the night as
we walked hand in hand with such inner delight. And
we'd hum, and we'd cling, as together we'd sing all
the love songs we'd heard from Sinatra or Bing.

Ah, those innocent, wonderful, old-fashioned times,
we were young, our hearts full of the musical lines
we would croon to each other from movies we'd seen,
but it's time to awake...was it only a dream?

Soup, Soup!

May 21, 2011

Soup, Soup, incontestable Soup,
reassuringly nourishing, flourishing Soup.
With desire on fire, begin with élan,
and combine the ingredients well in a pan,
or entrust, if you must, your desire to a can.

If in any event, your desire you must vent,
and you have nothing else, with a can be content.
But much better by far, to just jump in the car,
to the green-grocer hie, it can't be very far.
Only keep the Soup plain, please resist caviar.

But the Soup, ah, the Soup, the whole room permeate,
what sweet blending it's sending, how long must we
wait?
Resist lifting the lid, lest it evaporate,
my desire is so troubling, denial I hate,
I just have to have bubbling Soup on my plate.

Here it comes, here it is, oh, I have it at last,
terminating unbearable, terrible fast,
my cruel deprivation is finally past.
Ah, sublimely delicious, for this Soup I could die,
I'm so fully content, I've left room for some pie.

Struggling Poets

August 9, 2011

Our poets see beyond today
with dreams that strike a spark.
Their vision sweeping fog away
Revealing truth in all they say,
if men would only hark.

God's poets ever, in the past
revealed sweet revelation.
Whether men of intellect
or simple men, as we suspect,
who rose above their station.

Most seem revolutionary,
strangely out of step.
Marching to a different drummer,
hot in winter, cold in summer,
seemingly inept.

And so they move within our ranks,
though very few in number.
Speaking truth as on they toil,
the butt of jokes, dissenters foil,
deprived of lovely slumber.

So if you should a poet meet and
note his sad demeanour. Staggered
gait with eyes downcast, looking
like he'll never last,
don't laugh, he's just a dreamer.

Sweet Honey

July 12, 2010

I wandered out upon the way,
where fields of happy daisies play,
to sprightly dance and look about,
communicating there without
the slightest voice to scarce suggest,
response to bumblebee's request
to openly access sweet treasure,
preserved by daisies all together
deep within their virgin hearts,
where bees intrude by fits and starts,
to probe and search for treasure deep,
so tirelessly, no time for sleep,
for hungry hive at home awaits
the stream of bees through open gates,
as endlessly their treasure bring,
then ceaselessly on golden wing,
depart again for treasure trove,
as over countryside they rove,
working tirelessly for man,
to sweeten us, a lovely plan.
While daisies, after giving all,
must perish with approaching fall.
This whole arrangement's just for us,
they sacrifice without a fuss.

The daisies beautify our field,
then to the bees their treasure yield.
Sweet honey trove, our happy fate,
while all we have to do is wait.

Talking Raven

February 26, 2011

The Raven and the Crow are very clever birds you
know,
the stories of their antics and intelligence abound.
Why, 'twas only yesterday, when just to pass the time
away,
I was seated at a table in the plaza, near the sound.

When suddenly to my surprise and right before my
very eyes,
a bold and clever Raven joined me on the other chair.
Then with a curtsey or a bow, I couldn't be quite sure
somehow,
he casually mentioned that in passing, saw me sitting
there.

Now, I was taken quite aback, when he revealed his
name was Jack,
and after introductions, said how nice that we could
meet.
I feel, he said, I should defer, from lunching with you,
noble sir,
but good taste dictates ignoring you would be most
indiscreet.

You find me, sir, a little short, but I could tell that
you're a sport.
I'd be delighted if my presence entertained.
We could share a joint of beef, 'twould give my
appetite relief,
you'd be nothing lost and I'd enormously have gained.

Now it was just about this point, I discreetly scanned
the joint,
but saw that no one noticed anything amiss.
I was speechless you can tell, but Black Jack got on
very well,
this bird could talk, I never heard a bird like this.

I thought I'd better play along, not make a fuss in all
this throng,
called the waiter, placed an order for us both.
Jack said he's glad he hadn't heard me order oven-
roasted bird,
I ordered beef while Jack distinctly ordered toast.

When our meal was near its end, I noticed seated, an
old friend,
at a table that was very near to mine.
A ventriloquist I know, his voice expertly did he throw,
and as Jack left, the cheeky bird, exclaimed that dinner
was superb,
he'd love to stay, but that he mustn't waste his time.

Television Hellevision

January 08, 2010

There's something that's been troubling me for quite a
little while,
I've noticed on the telly, there isn't much to see.
Although my search is endless, as I turn that little dial,
the television I observe is entertainment free.

The T.V. guide informs me, there's a show called
Comedy,
but the comic uses language that turns the air to blue.
The ladies in the audience, all laugh coquettishly,
they really feel uncomfortable, don't know what else
to do.

Or situation comedies, all the good ones went away,
now
including cursing that would turn the air to blue.
Entertainment level's lowered, perversion's here to
stay,
There's not much intellectual, for a normal man to
view.

But then I found an interviewer, name of Charley Rose,
great guests at prime time evening, I watched him
every day.

Then they changed him to the afternoon, to two
o'clock would you suppose,
men all at work while mothers and their children are
at play.

Late afternoons and evenings are filled with games
inane,
or shocking revelations of the current movie stars.
Mind-numbing, time-consuming, they could send a
man insane.
If Charley's gone, you'll find me on next rocket ship to
Mars.

The Brain

October 11, 2011

The brain as an organ is chief,
it affords other organs relief.
Sends out orders all day,
while at work or at play,
and while sleeping, it's absence is brief.

A man's brain has a serious flaw,
which after I married, I saw.
Can't decipher a wife,
thus eliciting strife,
pursued, by a rude tooth and claw.

If ones brain takes its leave, maybe theft,
the commander in charge having left.
I've seen folks, it would seem,
walk around in a dream,
these are some who of brains are bereft.

While some others, their wiring seems dead,
some fuses keep blowing, it's said,
traffic lights are confusing,
not very amusing,
they think they should go on the red.

There are poets seen acting sublime,
who keep sending out missives in rhyme.
In a quite measured gait,
They will communicate,
They can't help but afflict all the time.

In my case, I'm not one who complains,
I misheard when they handed out brains.
I was last in the line,
didn't get there in time,
and missed out when I thought they said trains.

The Sweet Bye and Bye

November 2, 2011

Have you ever wondered what happens,
like, how long after you die?
Does your spirit man keep on hanging around,
as they're lowering your body into the ground,
are you hovering there nearby?

Like, when everyone slowly disperses,
do you follow one person away?
You can't follow them all,
you'd be much too small,
to put on that fancy display.

And anyway, no one could see you,
would not even know you were there.
Would you check out who's sad,
or who's secretly glad,
and more focused on what people wear?

Would you fly over to the reception,
just to check out the lay of the land.
You can't touch all that food,
you'd create quite a mood,
if a crepe left a plate with no hand.

Would you casually mix with the people,
just to hear how they speak of the dead?
One hand cupping your ear,
to see what you might hear,
while you're circling over their head.

And then when they all have departed,
that would leave you with nothing to do.
They'd all go to their homes,
perhaps reading your poems,
while debating what happened to you?

But at last you will make that long journey,
up there in the sweet bye and bye.
Flying with great élan,
as only you can,
to your mansion up high in the sky.

Titus and Ollie

May 16, 2011

Pup Titus and Ollie
Two buddies by golly
Entertained in a house called "Busy"
They both frolicked together
No matter the weather
Ensconced in their master's Tin-Lizzie

Now Ollie, by golly
By car, bus, or trolley
Would venture out any old day
When they take out the trash
He'd be off in a flash
He'd be sure to lead Titus astray

Now, as little dogs go
He's a pretty good Joe
But he'd wander, beyonder, away
Then pup Titus would follow
With a gulp and a swallow
They'd revel in freedom all day.

One day poor old Ollie's
Personality, by golly's
Was summarily detached by the Vet

Though he searched far and near
He won't find it I fear
Though he keeps looking back for it yet

Then the puppy called Titus
With a dance to delight us
Cavorted round Ollie that day
Please don't worry, old friend
You will mend in the end
And forget what the Vet took away

To Rhyme or Not to Rhyme

April 21, 2011

Well here I am at the keyboard again,
halfway through my eighty-fifth year.
And try as I might when I'm starting to write,
rhyming happens, just why isn't clear.

Oh, I really do try to be ever so sly,
and creep up on this page from the rear.
But as hard as I try, and I'm not gonna lie,
it just keeps on rhyming, how drear.

It's a terrible curse, and it keeps getting worse,
do you think something's wrong in my brain?
I see rhyming unravel as two fingers travel,
the keyboard again and again.

I must find some ploy, to this rhyming destroy,
I think I know what I must do.
Though it does sound absurd, I'll use any old word,
that last verse, I'll now write it anew.

Here we go...
It's a terrible curse, and it keeps getting bad,
Do you think something's wrong in my arm?
I see rhyming unravel as my two fingers poke
the keyboard again and... Stop! This is a joke.

That experiment suffered a terrible fate,
as you saw when you read my rewrite.
My fate seems to be, I'm sure you'll now agree,
to rhyme every time I write.

To the Death

September 1, 2012

To life or death
Tongue's powers lie
By which no writer
Canst deny
Unknowingly
His heart doth bare
Truth he believes
Tho unaware
His heart is opened
To the stare
Of unkind critic
Everywhere
If this he knew
Wouldst yet he care

Think not that he
Might careful be
Persuadeth
Most assuredly
He'd rather sever
Hand or head
Than change one word
Of what he's said
Standeth he then
To the death

And tho he draweth
His last breath
His treasure guard
Defiantly

Two Left Feet

November 23, 2012

What I'm lacking in aplomb
I make up with intensity
Determined not to then become
Within a crowd, the only one
Devoid of that propensity

Affecting a quite casual stance
With confidant composure
Offhandedly invite to dance
This lady with a studied glance
At formal gown's exposure

Pretending not to notice though
But feeling ill at ease
I trip as we begin to go
Then grin at her as down below
I'm tearing off her sleeve

Clambered quickly to my feet
Still keeping my composure
Glaringly with accent sweet
She promptly knocked me off my feet
I knew the dance was over

Vagabond Henry the Cat

August, 2009

Sweet Henry, my friend,
we were so happy when
we were told to Seattle
you've strayed.

When you left Toronto
we all did not want to
believe with some hussy you'd stayed.

So you'll understand why
we all had a good cry,
we had witnessed, we thought, your demise.

But now we're just fine
because we saw your sign
on Seattle's Best Coffee...how nice.

We're no longer afraid,
man, have you got it made
In the shade...eating western mice.

But now gone is your picture, it did
really depict your appearance, your
story's gone too.

Ah, fame is so fleeting,
perhaps we'll be meeting,
anon, when you start life anew.

And so, vagabond Henry,
when you land, you must send me
a card...don't end up in a zoo.

Water Abundant

September 29, 2012

Have you ever thought about water,
how important the stuff really is?
If you'd really consider the stuff as you aughter,
you would realize that the poor sea otter, must regard
the oceans as his.

And all of the water that ever was or evermore shall
be,
will now and forever more be contained
in this absorbable planet God has framed,
in one form or another it's rearranged,
though most of it lies in the sea.

Some of it though, in each of us lies,
though it's not too easy to see.
It goes back to the earth when one of us dies,
or becomes apparent when somebody cries,
or when somebody goes for a pee.

Sloshing around inside somewhere, you soak it up like
a blotter.
About seventy percent of your brain is wet,
which might explain why some people get,
water on the brain, but they never forget
to think quite well under water.

But enough of all of this technical stuff,
I just thought of some thankful solutions.
A sorry lot we all would be,
we would all be failures socially,
without our daily ablutions.

West Coast Sun

May 31, 2012

A curtain drab, if I may say
is drawn across the sky.
A glum unprepossessing slab
of sodden gray that seems to grab
the brightest part of May.

To fatally instill a gloom
depressingly so grey,
postponing then, the presence soon
of sunshine in my little room
to sweep the gloom away.

That cloudy ceiling hanging there
prevents, I surely know.
Sun's warm, enchanting love affair
that annually bestows the care
our gardens need to grow.

Here comes the sun, here comes the sun,
our growing thirst to slake.
I cannot be the only one
whose enthusiasm seems to run
the other way, when viewing hoe and rake.

Ah, thank God for the brightening days
we always knew would come.
Those life-enabling sunny rays,
despondence flees, enchantment plays
in happy hearts of gardeners, every one.

What If

April 29, 2012

Have you ever pondered the consequence
of choices made long past?
Of how your future was formed by chance,
with nary a slightest backward glance,
while life flew by so fast.

What if the war that ended too soon
for a lad who could never die,
had continued to decimate human lives,
would I be one who by luck survives,
without knowing the reason why?

Or the girl I courted who turned me down
and then married that other boy.
If she'd chosen me, would I ever rue
as father of seven instead of two,
a life I might never enjoy?

And then education, which I now lack,
would that have exalted my life?
Would the halls of learning have rescued me
from the limited intellect you now see,
and a lifetime of labor and strife?

So the premise with which this missive began,
holds merit as you can see.
Whatever would all of our lives be like,
would you drive a car while I pedal a bike,
or would I replace irreplaceable you,
and you, irreplaceable me?

What Time Is It?

August 16, 2012

My mind as I age
Or perhaps
I mean brain
Has a bad habit lately
Both time and again
Of remembering clearly
The second world war
The dinner I ate
Or the jacket I wore
But completely forgot
To know what
To call you
Although we've been
Married since 1902
Now we both know
Of course
That I do know your name
But what seems to be worse
I have no one to blame
Because just as I start
My recriminating
I forget what you said
That was so irritating
So I ask for a coffee
And you acquiesce

But when you bring toffee
I'm happy I guess
But you know I like chocolate
I wish you'd remember
By the way is this April
Or early September

What's in a Name?

September 21, 2012

With the advent of fame,
then obscurity's lost.
So what's in a name,
that is worth the cost?

With privacy gone, with
no hope of relief. This
smothering throng, one
would hope is brief.

Fame has its rewards,
I've heard it said.
But it moves one toward,
a certain dread.

Your friends all change, and you do too.
Life's grand rearrange,
in the end, has you.

Then you long for the days,
you could go for a walk.
When no one delays,
with desire to talk.

Let me tell you the cause,
of this obdurate lecture.
It's really because,
this is all conjecture.

For I'm no one, you see,
whom the crowds would seek.
I just happen to be,
full of gall and cheek.

Winter Rules

January 4, 2013

Bedroom window open wide
We cuddle under quilt
Winter winds regale outside
Filling me with guilt
Landlord turns the heat way down
Regards me as his rental clown
One day he'll chase me out of town
With blunderbuss he built

Wifey says she's freezing cold
She has to learn to cope
Fresh air's healthy I was told
Together we'll be growing old
That's if we both survive the cold
And landlord don't go broke

Wisdom Would Propose

September 1, 2012

It's early morn, unkempt, forlorn,
husband leaving, good-bye dear,
children waking, get in gear.
Dress them, feed them, scoot them off,
don't forget Mom's kiss so soft.
Off they go, the five of them,
meet them later on and then,
Mom has to do it all again.

Dad's gone to work, it's very far,
that's why Daddy has the car.
Nailed to insurance desk till five,
when he gets home he's half alive.

Quick, the bathroom, hurry, fuss,
half an hour to catch the bus,
off to work, our mommy goes,
head full of thoughts 'bout kids and clothes.
Plans her day and plans her night,
lunch hardly leaves time for a bite,
Mom rushes home, to kitchen led,
cook the supper, get them fed,
fall exhausted into bed.

Good night sweetheart, I love you dear,
sweet words she didn't want to hear,
his arm enfolds her, snuggles in,
from deep in sleep, rejecting him.
A warning sir, if thou be wise,
I understand and sympathize,
thy midnight plans do not impose,
thou'd better let thy lady doze,
wisdom strongly doth propose.

Why Me?

December 11, 2012

We're born
We dance
We look askance
We wonder why
The years
Fly by
They passed
They flew
When next
We knew
Surprised to find
We're fifty-two
Cannot deny
Again
We turn
We're still alive
But bordering
On eighty-five
To never fly
Before we die
But tell me why

My Underground Home

August 20, 2011

When at last I lie,
'neath the open sky,
in my new subterranean home.
I know that I'll grin,
while observing how thin,
my miserable shanks have grown.

I'll recline at my ease,
as relaxed as you please, with
no one creating a din. And as
hard as they try, though they
beg and they cry, I'm not
going to let them in.

I'll not pay any rent,
and I'm likely to vent
any spleen that is in me yet.
In my underground home,
where the beetles roam,
I'll have uttered my last epithet.

Oh, I'll wiggle and squirm,
might converse with a worm,
on the merit of this and that.
I won't feel any pain,

or get wet from the rain,
so I won't need my waterproof hat.

While I rest in my bunk,
tuned to the last trump,
all prepared for my journey on high.
When I hear it I'll know,
I'll be leaving below,
for my heavenly home in the sky.

Look for other volumes from
poet Bob McCluskey's prolific pen:

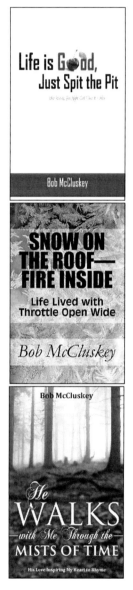